The Nature Kid's Guide to
WARTHOGS

DAVID ANDERSON

LP Media Inc. Publishing
Text copyright © 2026 by LP Media Inc.

For information address LP Media Inc. Publishing,
30012 Variolite St NW, Princeton MN 55371
www.lpmedia.org

Publication Data

Warthogs
The Nature Kid's Guide to Warthogs — First edition.

Summary: "Learn all about Warthogs, the Nature Kid Way"
— Provided by publisher.

ISBN: 979-8-89818-222-9

[1. Warthogs – Non-Fiction] I. Title.

Title: The Nature Kid's Guide to Warthogs

CONTENTS

SAVANNA SPOTS

Snort! A warthog trots across the sunny grassland.

Warthogs are not the most beautiful animals in Africa. But what they lack in looks, they more than make up for in toughness, speed, and character.

These stocky, thick-skinned animals live across the grassy **savannas** of Africa, where wide open land stretches in every direction. The open ground helps them spot danger coming from far away. The grass feeds them. The rivers cool them down.

They thrive in one of the most dangerous places on Earth, surrounded by lions, leopards, and hyenas every single day. And somehow they are doing just fine.

AFRICAN HOME

Warthogs have been spotted nearly two miles above sea level on Mount Kilimanjaro — one of Africa's highest mountains!

Thump! A warthog stomps through the dry African dirt.

Warthogs live in the southern half of Africa, below the huge Sahara Desert. They roam through over 30 countries!

Common warthogs are found in the most places. They like grasslands from Kenya to South Africa and stay near water when they can.

Desert warthogs live in East Africa. You can find them in Kenya, Ethiopia, and Somalia. These tough pigs do well in drier spots where other animals struggle.

SIZE CHECK

A warthog's big head can be one-third the length of its entire body!

Whomp! A big warthog plops into the soft, cool mud.

Warthogs are about as tall as a big dog. They stand around two feet high at the shoulder. Their bodies are round and strong.

A grown male can weigh up to 250 pounds! Females are lighter, around 150 pounds. Both are very powerful for their size.

A warthog's body stretches about four feet long. Its head is wide and flat, with small eyes peeking out from high on its face. That high eye placement helps them watch for danger while grazing.

WACKY WARTS

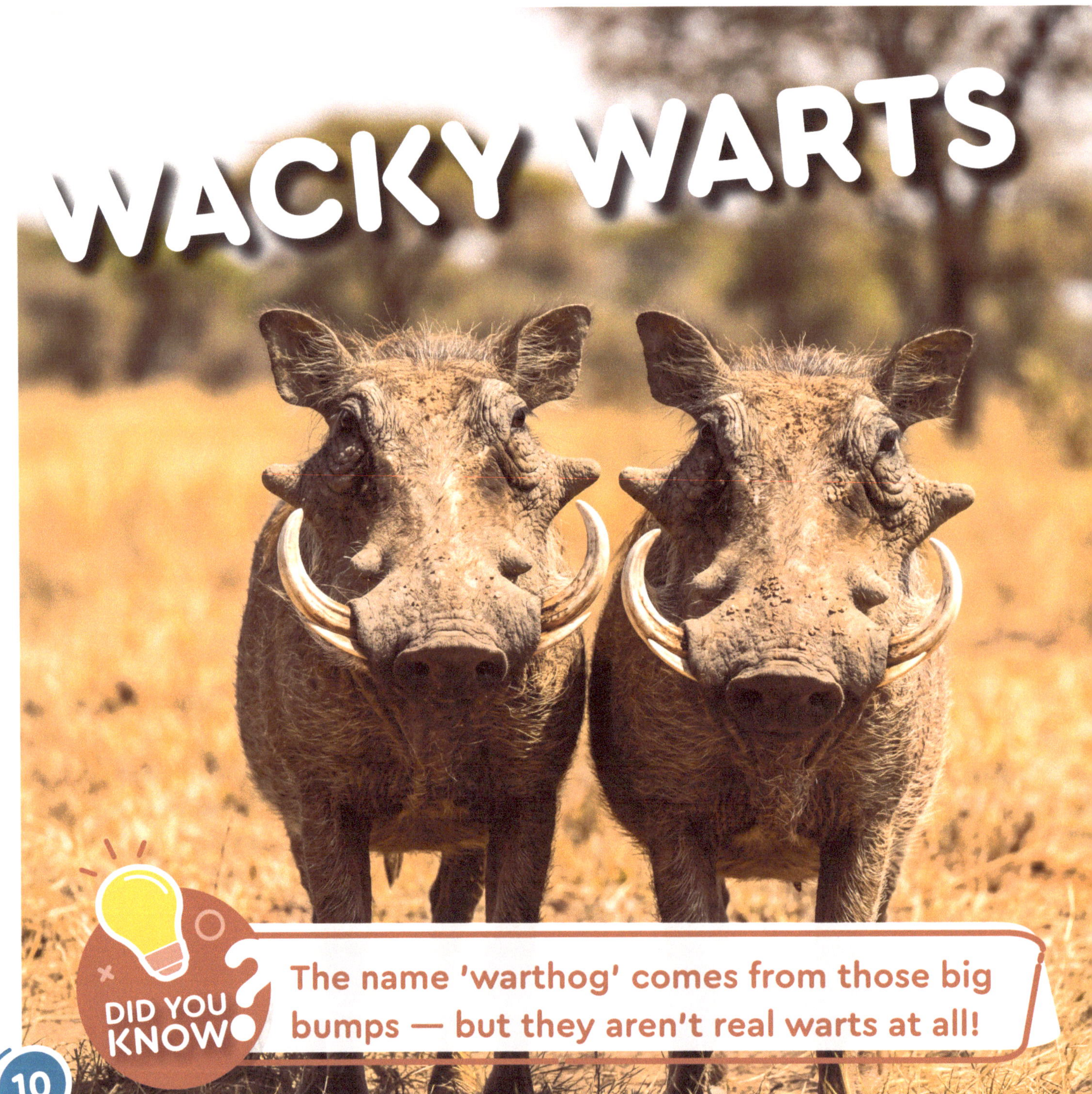

The name 'warthog' comes from those big bumps — but they aren't real warts at all!

Bonk! Two warthogs bump their tusks as they stand together.

Warthogs have big bumps on their faces. People call these bumps warts, but they are not real warts! They are thick pads of tough skin.

These bumps help keep a warthog's face safe. They work like soft cushions under the skin and can take a lot of hard knocks during fights.

Males have four large bumps on their face, sitting in two pairs on each side. Females have a smaller set. The bigger the bumps, the older the warthog!

SUPER SNIFFERS

Sniff, sniff! A warthog pokes its nose into the grass.

Warthogs have a very strong sense of smell. Their flat nose sniffs out food buried in the dirt. They can smell danger from far away too.

Their hearing is excellent as well. Big ears on top of the head catch many sounds. A warthog can hear a lion creeping through the grass long before it gets close.

But their eyes are not so great. Warthogs cannot see very far, so they count on their nose and ears instead. Those senses keep them alive.

TOUGH TUSKS

A warthog's tusks never stop growing — they can add several inches each year!

14

Clash! A warthog swings its sharp tusks at a hyena.

Warthogs have two pairs of **tusks**. The top tusks curve up and out like hooks. The bottom tusks are shorter but razor sharp.

Tusks are really long, curved teeth. Warthogs use them to dig up roots and fight off enemies. A male's upper tusks can grow over two feet long!

When danger comes, a warthog lowers its head and points its tusks right at the enemy. Not many animals want to face those sharp points!

GRUB GRAB
DID YOU KNOW?
Warthogs have thick, leathery pads on their knees from all that kneeling!
16

Crunch! A warthog chomps down on a fat, juicy root.

Warthogs spend a lot of time looking for food. They eat mostly grass and plants. In dry months, they dig up roots and bulbs hiding underground.

To eat grass, warthogs do something funny — they get down on their knees! They bend their front legs and shuffle along. This lets them reach short grass close to the ground.

Warthogs also eat bark, fruit, and even bugs. They are not picky at all. When food runs low, they eat almost anything they can find.

GRUNT TALK

Grunt, grunt! A mother warthog calls to her babies.

Warthogs make many sounds to talk to each other. They grunt softly when they eat as a group. Soft grunts mean all is well.

A scared warthog lets out a loud squeal. This warns the group that danger is near! The whole group may run when they hear it.

Warthogs also snort when they feel upset. Males growl at each other during fights. Each sound tells the group something important.

Scientists have counted at least seven different warthog calls, from soft grunts to loud alarm squeals!

HUNGRY HUNTERS

Baby warthogs face the most danger — only about half survive their first year!

Roar! A lion charges. A warthog runs to hide.

Life is not easy for warthogs on the savanna. Many big animals want to eat them, so they must always watch for danger.

Lions are their biggest enemy. Leopards, hyenas, and wild dogs hunt them too. Even big eagles may swoop down and grab a baby warthog.

Cheetahs chase young warthogs across the plains. Crocodiles snap at them near rivers. With so many hunters around, warthogs keep a sharp lookout every single day.

BURROW BOLT

Warthogs can squeeze into aardvark burrows that go 10 feet deep and have several rooms!

Zoom! A warthog dashes backward into its dark burrow.

When danger comes, warthogs run for a **burrow**. They do not dig their own holes. Instead, they use tunnels made by aardvarks and other animals.

Warthogs do something very clever at a burrow. They back in tail first, so their tusks face out! No hunter wants to reach in and get poked by those sharp points.

A family may use many burrows in their home area. They switch between them to stay safe and keep enemies guessing where they sleep.

ZOOM FAST

DID YOU KNOW?

24

Whoosh! A warthog zooms across the field, tail held high.

Warthogs are fast runners for their size. They can hit speeds of 30 miles per hour! That is as fast as a car driving through a neighborhood.

A running warthog sticks its thin tail straight up like a little flag waving. This helps the group stay together in tall grass.

Most of the time, warthogs trot along with tails down. But when they sense danger, up goes the tail! Then they take off as fast as they can, zigzagging to escape.

MUDDY DAYS

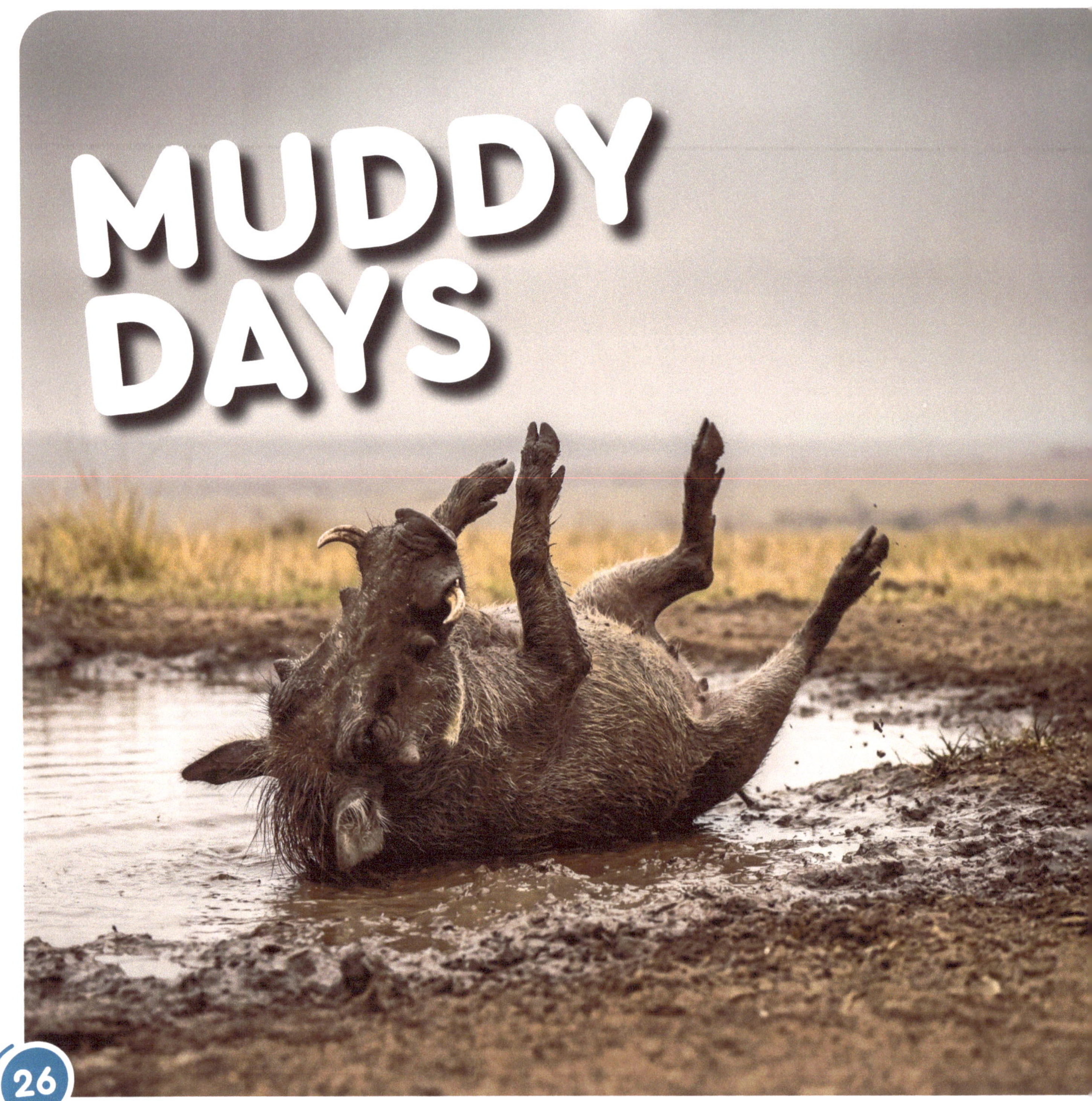

Squish! A warthog rolls in a thick patch of cool mud.

Warthogs are active during the day. They wake up when the sun comes up and head out to find food and water.

A mud bath is a big part of every day! Rolling in mud keeps pesky bugs away. The cool mud also feels great under the hot African sun.

As the sun goes down, warthogs head back to their burrow. They tuck in for the night deep underground, where it is dark and cozy.

Mud dries on a warthog's skin and works like natural sunscreen and bug spray combined!

SOUNDER SQUAD

Warthogs in a sounder sometimes pile on top of each other when they sleep!

Oink! A group of warthogs trots together toward water.

A group of warthogs is called a **sounder**. Sounders are made up of mothers and their young. They stick close together for safety.

Most sounders have four to eight members. The group eats, rests, and travels together. Someone always stands guard while the others feed.

Males usually live on their own. They join a sounder only when it is time to mate. Young males leave the group when they grow up and start their solo life.

TUSK TUSSLE

A male warthog is called a boar and a female is called a sow — just like farm pigs!

Crack! Two male warthogs slam their big heads together.

Male warthogs fight to win a mate. They push their heads together hard! The thick bumps on their faces soften the blows.

Two males may circle each other and grunt. Then they crash head to head, over and over. These fights look scary, but the warts protect them from real harm.

The winning male gets to stay near the females. He may follow a sounder for a few days. After that, he wanders off on his own again.

PIGLET PARADE

A warthog piglet doubles its weight in just two weeks — growing faster than most baby animals!

Squeal! Tiny warthog piglets tumble out of their burrow.

Baby warthogs are called piglets. A mother may have two to four babies at once. They are born inside a safe, warm burrow.

Piglets are tiny at birth. Each one weighs only about one pound — that is lighter than most newborn puppies!

At first, the piglets cannot see very well. But they can walk within just a few hours. After about a week, they follow their mother outside to explore the world.

MOM KNOWS

A mother warthog will charge a lion to protect her young — even though lions are five times her size!

Snuffle! A mother warthog sniffs her young piglet.

A mother warthog works hard to raise her piglets. She keeps them inside the burrow at first. This protects them from the hot sun and hungry hunters.

The mother feeds her babies with rich milk. She only leaves to find food and water for herself, but she always comes back quickly.

After a few weeks, the piglets go outside. Mom teaches them how to find food and shows them which plants are good to eat. She is their guide to the savanna.

TOUGH SURVIVORS

Huff! A desert warthog treks across the hot, dry land.

Warthogs are tough animals built for hard times. In dry months, food and water are hard to find. But warthogs have tricks to get by.

They can go many days without a drink. They get moisture from the roots and plants they eat. Their bodies are built to save every drop of water.

Warthogs handle scorching days and chilly nights. Their burrows keep them warm when temperatures drop. These smart pigs survive year after year, no matter what nature throws at them.

WARTHOG WATCH

Grunt! A warthog trots across its zoo habitat with its tail straight up in the air.

You do not have to travel to Africa to see a warthog up close. Many zoos across the United States keep warthogs, and they are always a crowd favorite.

When you visit, watch how they kneel down to eat, listen for their grunts and snorts, and look closely at those incredible tusks. Ask a keeper when feeding time is for the best view.

Look out for the warthog's tail too. When they run, they hold it straight up like a little flag — one of the funniest sights in any zoo!

GLOSSARY

savanna

A wide, flat grassland with few trees, found in warm places.

burrow

A hole or tunnel in the ground where an animal lives.

sounder

A group of warthogs that live and travel together.

tusks

Long, curved teeth that stick out of an animal's mouth.

boar

A male warthog; also used for male pigs